INTERACTIVE **WORKBOOK**

THE 'GROOMING' MYSTERY™

Unmasking the Sex Offender

Thank you to Theresa Harvard Johnson and Nancy E. Grabe for their contribution to *The Grooming Mystery*.

BOOKLOGIX
Alpharetta, GA

The resources contained within this book are provided for informational purposes only and should not be used to replace the specialized training and professional judgment of a healthcare or mental healthcare professional. Angela's Voice and the publisher of this work cannot be held responsible for the use of the information provided. Always consult a licensed mental health professional before making any decision regarding treatment of yourself or others.

Copyright © 2013, 2023 by Angela's Voice

Second Edition

All rights reserved. No part of this book may be reproduced or transmitted in any form or by any means, electronic or mechanical, including photocopying, recording, or any information storage and retrieval system, without permission in writing from the author.

ISBN: 978-1-61005-987-9

This ISBN is the property of BookLogix for the express purpose of sales and distribution of this title. The content of this book is the property of the copyright holder only. BookLogix does not hold any ownership of the content of this book and is not liable in any way for the materials contained within. The views and opinions expressed in this book are the property of the Author/Copyright holder, and do not necessarily reflect those of BookLogix.

∞ This paper meets the requirements of ANSI/NISO Z39.48-1992 (Permanence of Paper)

Workbook text by Theresa Harvard Johnson, Nancy E. Grabe, Angela Williams.
Design and Illustration by Mark Sandlin.
Design production by Felicia Kahn.

051023

CONTENTS

Introduction _____ 1

How Perpetrators Gain Access to Children: The Grooming Mystery _____ 5

Who is a Groomer? _____ 7

Commonly Identified Characteristics of Adult Sex Offenders _____ 13

Groomer Techniques _____ 13

Circumstances and Environments Commonly Employed by Offenders _____ 20

Sexual Exploitation of Children _____ 20

Protecting Our Children From Grooming _____ 24

Things To Look For in a Potential Child Sexual Abuse Offender _____ 27

Possible Signs a Child is being 'Groomed' _____ 29

Child Sexual Abuse Prevention _____ 30

Define Online Solicitation by Predators _____ 31

A Modern Day Predator Phenomena _____ 32

Internet 'Grooming' Behaviors _____ 33

Possible Signs Your Child is Being 'Groomed' Via the Internet _____ 35

Instant Messaging Abbreviations _____ 37

Internet 'Grooming' Prevention and Protection _____ 37

Internet 'Grooming' Intervention _____ 39

Disclosure-Understanding the Process _____ 40

    Calmly Receiving a Disclosure _____ 41

    Following a Disclosure _____ 41

    Be Aware and Prepare _____ 41

    Child Advocacy Centers _____ 42

    Resources _____ 43

Angela's Voice _____ 44

Join the Angela's Voice Movement _____ 46

INTRODUCTION

There is absolutely nothing more important to parents than securing the safety of their children. It is second nature to teach them to watch for cars before crossing the street and to not accept rides from strangers at any time. We encourage them to tell us if they are being bullied in the schoolyard or on the playground; and how to refuse the offer if they are confronted or pressured into using alcohol, other drugs or household inhalants. While training our children in these areas is critical, routine and ongoing, there is one very significant area that is often overlooked: the dangers of child sexual abuse.

At Angela's Voice, a leading national organization dedicated to child sexual abuse awareness, prevention, and healing, our goal is to ensure that every parent knows the risks to their child and is prepared to stand vigilantly in awareness and prevention. In the United States, it is common for parents or even children to believe that they are safe and outside of the reach of anyone who would choose to sexually assault them. A few common myths noted by researchers from the Centers for Disease Control & Prevention, The National Child Traumatic Stress Network and others include:

- Believing that child sexual abuse is rare
- Believing that children are abused only by strangers
- Believing that child sexual abuse only affects certain social classes or demographic groups

This, however, could not be further from the truth. Many parents are not aware that there are an estimated 42 million survivors of child sexual abuse in the United States and 1 in 4 girls and 1 in 6 boys will be sexually abused before their 18th birthday. To bring this truth home, this means that out of four children whom a person may know or see together at any given time, one of those children will be or has already been sexually abused.

Experts agree that the first line of defense in protecting children is to engage parents and caregivers. This engagement involves educating the parents, teaching parents how to train their children and aiding families to help build vigilant communities in which the subject of child sexual abuse is no longer taboo. In doing so, children will not fear disclosing their abuse and perpetrators will have nowhere to hide. This approach is significant because the actuality of the myths mentioned above is as follows:

> - Child sexual abuse is an epidemic in the United States
> - 93% of child sexual abuse cases are perpetrated by someone the child knows and trusts. For a parent or a caregiver, this means that a perpetrator could literally be anyone who has built a trusting relationship within the family unit – whether a relative or a close friend
> - Child sexual abuse happens in all social classes and demographic groups

The purpose of this book is simple: Angela's Voice wants to be a part of the process that gives parents and caregivers the tools they need to unravel the mystery behind child sexual abuse by helping them understand the risks, recognizing how child sexual abusers generally gain access to children and how they can help protect them. With this knowledge, child sexual abuse will not be a mystery since concerned individuals will be armed with the knowledge to help predict and prevent child sexual abuse.

MOTIVATED TO PROTECT

By exposing the issue of child sexual abuse and educating adults about the risks that every child faces, it is our hope that we will help create a safer, happier and healthier world. We believe that every adult is responsible for the safety of a child. The first step is simple: "Learn everything you can about child sexual abuse."

Do you know the facts about child sexual abuse and are you comfortable sharing this information to help educate your community?

- 1 in 4 girls will be sexually abused before their 18th birthday
- 1 in 6 boys will be sexually abused before their 18th birthday
- 70% of all sexual assaults are perpetrated against children under the age of 17
- Currently, only 1 of every 10 sexual abuse survivors will ever tell
- 93% of child sexual abuse cases are perpetrated by someone the child knows and trusts
- A Sex Offender molests, on average, 117 children before being caught, and can molest as many as 400 children
- There are an estimated 42,000,000 child sexual abuse survivors in the United States alone

Our goal is to do whatever we can to empower you to protect your child, our children.

Let's consider these numbers for a minute. Think of 6 people who live near you, whether you know them well or not. Write their names here:

_____   _____

_____   _____

_____   _____

Based on the statistics above, one person from your list could be a Child Sexual Abuse survivor. And, the abuse they suffered probably would have occurred prior to the age of 18. It is a stunning reality when you begin to take a mental survey of the numbers of people we encounter every single day who are survivors of child sexual abuse. Even more tragic is the personal and collateral damage that child sexual abuse causes in our world and that more is not being done to address this devastating problem. As you consider the people in this list, think about what could have been done to prevent these atrocities in their lives as you read through this workbook. Keep in mind that what you learn and put into action WILL help save a child.

PASSIONATE ABOUT CHANGING SOCIETAL ATTITUDES

Angela's Voice is working to bring about social and systemic changes in our world so our society becomes vigilant in protecting children from child sexual abuse. Several of these social changes include;

- Removing the stigma of child sexual abuse from the victims
- Giving this epidemic public visibility
- Promoting compassion, healing, resources and programs for survivors
- Educating adults about their need to take responsibility for the protection of all children. A trained, conscientious and vigilant society puts the predator on notice and gives the children a circle of safety to protect them

DREAMING BIG

Angela's Voice's dream is to create a vigilant society that will protect children from child sexual abuse. When children grow up with their emotional and physical boundaries protected, we create healthier adults. When healthier adults are raising the next generation of children, we create healthier generations.

> It is Angela's Voice's mission:
> - To end this silent epidemic
> - To live in a world where this plague of child sexual abuse is fully eradicated

A MOVEMENT WITH A MISSION

Angela's Voice is working hard to provide;

- Public awareness on the issue of child sexual abuse
- Prevention training to educate adults on how to predict and prevent child sexual abuse
- Aftercare healing and restoration programs in the community

Angela's Voice is dedicated to a movement to break the silence and cycle of child sexual abuse worldwide and we invite you to get involved in the movement.

HOW PERPETRATORS GAIN ACCESS TO CHILDREN:
THE GROOMING MYSTERY

We can never over stress how important it is to talk about child sexual abuse. This book, *The Grooming Mystery*, will help make this process easier as understanding comes forth. As you take this journey into learning more, please know that our efforts are not to create a paranoid society or to raise suspicion concerning every adult in our sphere of influence who takes an interest in a child. We are, however, providing parents and caregivers with some much needed information as well as prevention tools. As we walk through this topic together, we will emphasize revealing ways children are targeted and manipulated by their abusers.

We will answer this question for you: Who are these perpetrators and how do they get past loving concerned parents/guardians to abuse children?

We have all heard about Jerry Sandusky, the former Penn State defensive coordinator and founder of the Second Mile program for at risk children, being found guilty of 45 separate charges involving sexual assaults of 10 boys who participated in his program.

Judge John Cleland explained the risk faced by communities quite clearly in his statement at Sandusky's sentencing. Here is a small part of that statement:

6 THE GROOMING MYSTERY

> There is no dispute that you [Sandusky] have done much positive work in your career and in your community, and not just with the Second Mile. It is perhaps the ultimate tragedy of your situation that all the qualities that made you so successful as a coach and community leader have continued to conceal the very vices that have led to your downfall. And it is precisely that ability to conceal your vices – apparently from yourself and from everybody else – that makes you dangerous.
>
> You abused the trust of those who trusted you. These were not crimes committed against strangers. Those kinds of crimes are bad enough, but to betray the trust of those who looked to you as a protector is much, much worse.
>
> So the crime is not only what you did to their bodies. Your crime is also what your assault did to their psyches and to their souls; and your assault to the sense of safety and wellbeing of the larger community in which we all live. There is a lesson for our communities in all of this. It is that in the protection of our children we must always be vigilant to assure that there are not those among us who would harm them. The problem is that where pedophiles are concerned it is very often the case that they, as you were, are trusted community figures.
>
> It is hard for the average citizen to understand why pedophiles are not quickly recognized and caught. But the reality is that it is the very nature of the pedophile's method to take time to ingratiate himself to both parents and children – to develop relationships of trust that enable him first to commit his crimes, and then to conceal his crimes.
>
> (www.nydailynews.com/blogs/iteam/2012/10/judge-john-clelands-statement-on-jerry-sandusky-sentencing)

Think about this statement for a moment – Judge Cleland says the lesson for our communities is that we must be vigilant and remember that the very nature of pedophiles (child sexual offenders) is that they can and do conceal themselves in our communities.

The process child sexual offenders use to manipulate the children they abuse and the adults who believe they are protecting them is called Grooming or preparing them for a specific purpose. Sexual abusers prepare their children to trust them and be their victims. The grooming also includes gaining the trust of the adults in the children victims' lives, and the community at large.

'GROOMING' is the finely honed skill of manipulation, employed by a child sex offender in a CONSISTENT and DELIBERATE attempt to gain the TRUST of a child (and family), so to engage with the child for the ULTIMATE PURPOSE of SECURING SEXUAL CONTACT with that CHILD.

WHO IS A GROOMER?

We have all seen a movie about a con artist that takes advantage of someone's vulnerability to get something he wants. The victim may feel uncomfortable at first, but the con artist works him with manipulative skills, and creates a belief in the child that the con artist will protect him or meet his needs like no one else. Often the community is never aware of the crime that has been committed and the sexual offender is on to his next victim.

A child sex offender is a con artist and what he desires is sexual contact with a child. Just like the movie con artist, he looks for vulnerability in someone that has what he wants.

Children of the right age and sex for that specific predator are singled out, and then he looks for opportunity. Situations such as absent parents or children who have low self-esteem, or who are loners, make it easy for predators to involve themselves in the life of their target, presenting themselves as a special friend and/or protector. The process of grooming is

often slow and calculated. Predators are willing to take their time to make sure that they can count on the child not to talk and the adults not to notice.

Think about the characteristics of con artists: They are charming, helpful, trustworthy, and always there when their victim needs them. That would describe Jerry Sandusky. That would describe most child sexual abusers. They appear to be everything a child needs and they work hard to become their confidant and savior.

The Assistant Attorney General for the State of Wisconsin, Gregory M. Weber, specializes in crimes against children; he interviews criminals all the time. Here are a few quotes from the sexual abuse con artists to whom he has spoken:

> "Parents are so naive – they're worried about strangers and should be worried about their brother-in-law. They just don't realize how devious we can be. I used to abuse children in the same room with their parents and they couldn't see it or didn't seem to know it was happening."
>
> "I was disabled and spent months grooming the parents, so they would tell their children to take me out and help me. No one thought that disabled people could be abusers."
>
> "Parents are partly to blame if they don't tell their children about [sexual matters] – I used it to my advantage by teaching the child myself."
>
> "Parents shouldn't be embarrassed to talk about things like this – it's harder to abuse or trick a child who knows what you're up to."
> (www.vachss.com/guest_dispatches/grooming.html)

Those comments are terrifying, but they can be helpful if we are willing to listen and learn. We need to be knowledgeable so that we can protect our children, having learned from the offenders' own words.

It is easier to talk to our children about someone taking advantage of their trust like a con artist, a person who will trick them into trusting them, than the scary sexual abuser. We want to empower our kids, not frighten them. Your child might want to help you catch a con artist.

How might you use this information to talk with your child about people that are unsafe? _____

WHO ARE WE TALKING ABOUT?

The act of child sexual abuse is so heinous that we often refer to the offenders as predators, animals, or monsters. Although this may accurately describe their behavior, it also helps them to hide. If you are looking for a monster; you will overlook a helpful uncle or the wonderful coach, scout leader or the baby sitter none of whom may act or look like monsters! Language is so important; it affects the way we think and act. So let us refer to those grooming our children for sex as sex offenders.

> **"They may be more similar to the general population than different."**
>
> Understanding Sex Offenders: An Introductory Curriculum
> US Department of Justice

So who are we looking for? We have all watched a show or heard an expert on the news talk about profiling. Forensic and psychological experts have tried to create a single, accurate or usable child sex abuser profile that describes all predators, but with little success. Research repeatedly shows that they are from all walks of life and may be male or female, intellectual or below average in intelligence, employed or unemployed. Regardless of the characteristics or features studied, there is no one typical sex offender.

According to the Center for Sex Offender Management, there are a few behaviors that if changes over time have the potential to indicate sexual reoffending.

> **These behaviors are:**
> - Problems with intimacy, or conflicts in intimate relationships
> - Increased hostility
> - Emotional identification with children
> - Becoming preoccupied with sexual matters or activities
> - Lifestyle instability and self-regulation difficulties, such as employment problems, impulsivity, and substance abuse
> - Attitudes and beliefs that tend to support or justify criminal or antisocial behaviors
> - Demonstrating non-compliance with supervision or treatment expectations

Unfortunately, these are just possible predictors and not exact indicators. So if someone you know goes through a change in one or more of these areas of his life and personality, it may be best not to leave him alone with your child or children.

It may be a surprise to know that one of the single greatest indicators of a potential sexual predator is his language and attitude concerning crimes – sexual crimes in particular. When a remark is made suggesting a victim 'deserves' to be raped or 'brought it on herself', it should be considered serious.

> **There is no place in our culture for any attitude placing responsibility for child sexual abuse or rape onto the victim! There is nothing a victim does, says, looks like or wears to provoke a crime he or she 'deserves'. NOTHING!**

Language and attitudes to the contrary should be stopped. You can make the difference. Never allow this kind of speech. You might want to report a youth worker, coach or teacher that expresses this type of attitude or opinion to his superior.

If you have a friend or relative that shares these opinions, you might want to limit your contact with him and certainly never leave him alone with your child.

Have you or someone you know ever had attitudes or made remarks resembling the following? Have you heard any of these in recent headline cases of sexual abuse or rape?

- ☐ "Well, no wonder she was raped. She wears low cut tops and short skirts."
- ☐ "That kid behaves provocatively."
- ☐ "She shouldn't have been drunk at a party."
- ☐ "If a woman dresses like a piece of meat, she should expect the animals to want her."
- ☐ "He could have said 'no'!"
- ☐ "All the kid had to do was run away."
- ☐ "Well, a teenager is old enough to know better and tell."
- ☐ "It can't be rape. Everyone knows she's the town whore."
- ☐ "She said no, but she didn't fight so she asked for it."

> Teenagers can be sex offenders. Some common characteristics are listed below:
> - Ages range between 13 and 17
> - Tend to be Male
> - 30-60% exhibit learning disabilities and academic dysfunction
> - Up to 80% have a diagnosable psychiatric disorder
> - Many have difficulties with impulse control and proper judgment
> - 20-50% have histories of being physically abused
> - 40-80% have histories of being sexually abused (continuing the sexual abuse cycle)
> - Juveniles account for approximately 50% of Child Sexual Abuse (CSA) crimes

No one characteristic identifies someone as an offender. However, if a young person you know has several of the above characteristics, it may be best not to leave him alone with your child.

One thing is clear from the numbers: Juveniles who have been abused, particularly without having received professional counseling, are likely to become abusers. The first step to halting this cycle is to be aware and report any suspected abuse being perpetrated against a child. There are ways to report anonymously to child welfare agencies and law enforcement. Let us do our job of protecting children by reporting any suspicion to the proper agencies and let them do their job.

COMMONLY IDENTIFIED CHARACTERISTICS OF ADULT SEX OFFENDERS

The following behaviors and attitudes are commonly held among adult sexual criminals. Although there is no profile for child sexual offenders, the following behaviors and attitudes should be considered cause for concern when seen in teens or adults:

- Deviant sexual arousal, interest or preferences when compared to standard societal norms
- Difficulty or an inability to understand social rules and behavioral norms, and a lack of respect for the personal boundaries and safety of others
- Social, interpersonal and intimacy deficits; might be considered socially awkward
- Victim empathy deficits – the inability to sense the damage and consequences a victim of maltreatment would experience – does not view it as wrong
- Poor self-management skills and self-control
- Under-detected deviant sexual behaviors – often ignored or denied by those around the offender
- History of maltreatment or abuse, particularly if counseling or therapy were not received
- Hostility
- Crime-tolerant attitudes
- Anti-social personality and psychopathy
- Emotional identification with children
- Lifestyle instability

GROOMING TECHNIQUES

Researchers have found that child sexual offenders have deliberate tactics they use to select victims and engage them in sexual abuse. Forensic psychologist Dr. Michael Welner, has identified 6 stages of this grooming process which have been adapted by multiple organizations working to protect children.

Stage 1: Targeting

The offender looks for children with vulnerabilities. A good target might be an emotionally needy, isolated child or one with low self-esteem. Children with low parental involvement are often a target. Children with a history of behavior problems are potential targets because if they tell, adults are more likely to believe the helpful adult than the troubled youth. Children with language disorders who have no speech or limited speech are often targeted.

Even children from stable, happy, two parent families are at risk. They may be worried about growing up or fitting in and if the parents do not take the concern seriously, an offender might take advantage of these fears.

The happiest and healthiest children may have moments when they struggle with self-esteem and social status. Being vigilant and being a good listener to children's concerns will help protect them. Remember, children's concerns and fears can be acknowledged without agreeing that their emotions are valid. You do not have to say they are more than they are, just reassure them that they are "good enough" and you will help them through this rough patch.

Stage 2: Gaining Trust

This is a stage of patience; the offender watches and gets to know his intended victim. Offenders work to discover their intended victim's needs and how to best fill them. The offender will appear to be a responsible caregiver, showing great affection and attention. A savvy offender will learn to push himself into children's lives without revealing his true motive. Dr. Welner compares them to a spy, saying that they are just as stealthy, becoming the confidante of the child and learning what emotional, social and parental needs the child feels are being neglected. It is a sinister and calculated process, defiling boundaries and eliciting trust from the child who cannot know that the trusted person intends harm.

During this stage, offenders may introduce secrecy to build a tight relationship with the child.

Little secrets at first: Coach may let the boys swear in the locker room and tell them not to tell their parents because they would not understand; the babysitter lets the child stay up late or eat a forbidden snack, always telling him not to tell the parents. The offender creates trust with the child and starts to develop distance between the child and his parents. The secrets get bigger and more numerous, and the child's ability to talk with the parents diminishes.

It is important to teach your children not to keep secrets. Be careful you do not ask them to keep secrets; you may be teaching them inadvertently that it is okay. Make sure you tell them the difference between a surprise and a secret. You only keep a surprise secret for a little while (like a gift or a party) and that surprise makes someone happy. In contrast, a secret is intended never to be told and is often harmful. No one should ever ask a child to keep a secret. There is a difference between secrets and surprises; secrets are concealed, surprises get revealed!

Stage 3: Filling the Need

During this stage the offender grows in importance to the child. The offender meets the child's needs with gifts, affection or attention. The child may begin to idolize the offender and be proud of the status their relationship gives the child. By doing this, the offender is starting to create a need in the child to protect the offender and keep their relationship safe from others.

Often offenders just empathize with the child, recounting their own issues with the child's struggles. If a child feels like he is being treated like a baby, the offender may say, "I know how that feels; my parents never appreciated and respected me either. But I know how grown up you are and I will treat you better than they do! I really love you." Not only does this build up their relationship, but it starts to diminish the relationship with the protective parents. In the eyes of a child, having an adult be 'just like me' is very affirming and builds confidence and trust.

Watch for adults that start to shower your child with gifts or affection. Also keep a vigilant eye open for a growing importance of any one individual in your child's life outside the sphere of parents or guardians.

Stage 4: Isolation

The offender is working to get the child alone. He may offer to babysit for free or take the child on a special outing. The offender is using the alone time to reinforce his and the child's "special" connection. He is developing the idea in the child that he appreciates or loves the child more than any other adult, even the child's parents or guardians.

Be vigilant not to build up relationships with other adults too much. It is great that a sitter loves your child but never make it too big a deal or you may unintentionally help an offender. The intent is not to make you paranoid. Great loving sitters, teachers, adult friends or coaches are a gift. Just drop in unannounced periodically on a babysitter. Plan to never have your child alone with a coach or tutor. Teach your child to always have a couple of friends with him. The buddy system is a great protector.

Stage 5: Sexualizing the relationship

The offender will build on the relationship he has created with nonsexual touch. The offender will tickle, wrestle or accidentally touch the child. He may use discussions, pictures, bathing or swimming to desensitize his victim. Visible signs include:

- Accidental touching of non-sexual body parts
- Touching on the head, face, shoulders
- Making close contact in pools, athletics, etc.
- Volunteering for Bedtime activities
- Encouraging the child to sit on the (PREDATOR'S) lap close together
- Hair brushing
- Helping them put on outerwear
- Bathing
- Tickling
- Lying down on a couch or bed together
- Snuggling, sometimes under covers

Then the offender will take advantage of the child's natural curiosity and physical stimulation to introduce sexual touch. The offender will use the child's physical body responses to secure compliance. When an individual's body is stimulated sexually, a natural response occurs. This is not different for a child. However, he may confuse a positive physical response with several potentially conflicting emotions and internal messages. An offender will affirm these messages to elicit compliance:

"It feels good and natural; therefore it can't be bad"

"I must want this"

Most offenders take this opportunity to teach the child about sex and shape the child's preferences. As the offender develops the child's sexuality, the relationship is redefined as more special. The child may be conflicted about the sexual arousal or feel shame and fear, causing him to become more secretive.

Stage 6: Maintain Control

By this point, the child is completely entangled in the relationship. He is often fearful of losing the relationship which he believes to be so special, but can be afraid of it at the same time. The child's immaturity and confusion is expertly used by an offender who tells the child that if he gives up this relationship and is not believed by anyone, he will be more alone and unwanted than he was prior to this relationship. Some sexual offenders threaten to hurt or kill the child or the child's loved ones if he tells someone about what has occurred. The child is often trapped in a silent prison of pain and fear. Offenders use a full arsenal to get children to keep the secret.

Encouragement and Affirmation

Children who are starved for attention are more likely to be susceptible to being groomed by encouragement and affirmation.

"This touching is 'good' (or 'special') because our relationship is 'special'.
"Only 'special' friends share this kind of bond."

Comments like these are usually coupled with instructions to keep the abuse secret because others who are not as special or who do not share such a unique bond will not be able to understand. This interaction leaves the manipulated child believing he is the recipient of a treasured gift.

Verbal Reinforcement

"This is our little secret."
"Best friends keep each other's secrets."

Using negative messages can be another side of the offender's strategy. It may be used alone or in conjunction with the more affirming language. Some examples are:

Consequences ("If you tell...")

"I won't love you anymore."
"We won't be friends."
"I'll have to go away and won't be able to spend time with you anymore."

Fear and Intimidation ("If you tell...")

"You'll be in a lot of trouble."
"I'll hurt you (or someone/something you love)."
"No one will believe you."
"Your parents will leave you."
"You made me do this."

The offender may tell the child that their relationship is normal, that everyone does it, but they do not talk about it.

He may blame the child for allowing the relationship to happen in the first place. The offender may even further confuse the child by using several or all of these techniques. Children are not able to see that all of these statements are not true, and they fall into silent compliance out of fear and confusion, feeling alone and trapped.

Some offenders will use physical punishment to keep the child compliant. They will pinch or hold private parts too hard or push the child down so they can blame the marks on the fall. Offenders become experts at hiding or explaining away bruises. Occasionally, offenders will even tell parents or guardians 'stories' about misbehavior so the parent will discipline his child for not complying with the offender.

Be sure to ask lots of questions if your child is hurt. Ask the adult and your child separately. If the stories are different, there may be a problem. If an adult complains about your child listening or behaving, ask for examples. When you talk to your child, ask him about what he thought happened and then remind him to be polite but to let you know if he is ever asked to do something that makes him uncomfortable or that he thinks is wrong.

If the offender, for whatever reason, believes fear is the best 'grooming' tool, they will use power and intimidation, threats and physical harm to secure compliance from a child. Depending on the nature of the offender, the child and circumstances, fear may be the first line of behavior by a potential perpetrator. This is most likely to happen when the offender is living in the home of the child he seeks to sexually abuse. All family members, caregivers and others who already have relationships with the child's family may forgo any attempts at 'grooming' for trust and begin to use intimidation and threats to keep the child from resisting sexual advances or disclosing abuse.

An offender is likely to increase the frequency and intrusiveness of the sexual abuse over time.

Abuse of the child may progress to more perverse forms of sexual activity. For instance, from fondling to oral sex, then, from oral sex to penetration and so on.

CIRCUMSTANCES AND ENVIRONMENTS COMMONLY EMPLOYED BY OFFENDERS

One on One – one adult or older adolescent and one child (victim)

- This method is the most commonly employed by offenders of children
- According to The Teenage Sex Offender, by Howard Barbaree, teenagers are believed to perpetrate 50% of Child Sexual Abuse acts

GROUP – when more than one perpetrator or victim is involved

- Several child victims to one offender or several offenders to a single victim
- Multiple offenders and victims
- May include families or organizations (day care, athletic programs, youth services, organized crime rings and cults)

SEX RINGS – whose sole purpose is to perpetuate Child Sexual Abuse in larger numbers

- Generally organized by PEDOPHILES (a person whose primary sexual orientation is to children)
- Most often developed for profit
- May include sophisticated recruitment, child pornography and prostitution

SEXUAL EXPLOITATION OF CHILDREN

The majority of children exploited in the following ways were sexually abused one-on-one first.

- **Child pornography** – Child pornography is a form of child sexual exploitation and a federal crime carrying the possibility of statutory penalties. Federal law defines child pornography as any visual depiction of sexually explicit conduct involving a minor (persons under 18 years of age). Images of child pornography are also referred to as child sexual abuse images.

Emerging trends reveal an increase in the number of images depicting sadistic and violent child sexual abuse, and an increase in the number of images depicting very young children, including toddlers and infants. eGroups and Peer to Peer Networks (P2P) account for a large portion of child pornography trafficking and sharing online. The FBI has task forces assigned to each of these criminal sharing venues. According to the FBI's Innocent Images National Initiative, they saw a 2026% increase in cyber child pornography investigations between 1996 and 2005, just 9 years.

> "Unfortunately, we've also seen a historic rise in the distribution of child pornography, in the number of images being shared online, and the level of violence associated with child exploitation and sexual abuse crimes. Tragically, the only place we've seen a decrease is in the age of victims. This is – quite simply – unacceptable." (US Attorney speaking at the National Strategy Conference on Combating Child Exploitation in San Jose, CA, May 19, 2011)

Do you see a correlation between the rise of Internet child pornography and sexual abuse crimes against children? _____
_____
_____

What can you as a parent do to diminish your child's risk or exposure to these Cyber-crimes? _____
_____
_____

- **Child prostitution (trafficking)** – when money is exchanged for the sexual acts performed by a child

According to the FBI, child prostitution brings higher profits than trafficking adults. The rise of social media advertising has brought an increase in a predator's ability to attract and recruit children for the purpose of selling them sexually. The average age of a child prostitute, in the United States, is 12 years old and there are at least 400,000 being trafficked. Victims of child trafficking generally range in age between 11 and 17, and have been found to be as young as 18 months. They can be forced to perform 30 sex acts per day and most often do not leave because any attempts to do so would leave result in beatings or death. They are enslaved and cannot escape.

> What are some ways you can take a personal stance against child pornography and prostitution? _____
> _____
> _____
> _____

Here are a few examples of what you can do:

- Write your politicians and tell them you want funds designated to stop these plagues, and you want penalties increased for those who perpetrate them. Prevention programs need funding
- Stop purchasing from companies who use sexualized depictions of children and teens in their advertising. This further desensitizes the population to accept children as objects of sexual desire
- Write online companies who allow advertisements for sexual acts to be posted on their websites. Internet searches will give you many examples of companies that allow this behavior
- Encourage politicians and Federal agencies from arresting children for sex crimes. They are victims
- Educate yourself, your children and your community about the prevalence of these crimes

- **RITUAL ABUSE** – a particular belief system involving sex with children among its core tenets

According to the U.S. Department of Health and Human Services Child Welfare division:

- This is highly abusive physically, psychologically, emotionally, spiritually and sexually – entailing crimes often glorified in horror movies
- It is likely to include some form of Satanism or 'devil'/'god' worship, where acts of abuse are perpetrated as an 'offering' to a 'higher being'
- Perpetrators engage in 'ritual' acts of a highly sadistic nature, in part to indoctrinate children, prevent disclosure and as a tenet of their belief system
- This organized abuse most often employs the use of costumes, symbols, artifacts, bodily fluids, drugs, chants, 'religious' sites, etc.
- This abuse may involve torture, impregnation of menstruating female children, confinement, murder and dismemberment of humans and animals (for the sake of 'sacrifice')

This is not relegated to Third World countries. It happens in every country of the world. Pretending it does not exist is part of the challenge to bringing these crimes and their perpetrators to justice here in the United States.

CHILD SEXUAL ABUSE (CSA): A PLAGUE OF EPIDEMIC PROPORTIONS

U.S. Law Enforcement statistics tell us an Offender will commit sexual abuse acts an average of 117 times; 62 times prior to their first arrest.

Interviews, conducted by Emory University Psychiatrist, Dr. Gene Abel, that guaranteed complete confidentiality and immunity from prosecution, discovered that:

- Male offenders who abused girls had an average of 52 victims each
- Men who molested boys had an astonishing average of 150 victims each
- Only 3% of these crimes had ever been detected

(Sexual Assault of Young Children as Reported to Law Enforcement: Victim, Incident, and Offender Characteristics, by Howard N. Snyder, Ph.D.; National Center for Juvenile Justice, July 2000, U.S. Department of Justice, Office of Justice Programs)

What would you say contributes to the large number of victims a PREDATOR has prior to being arrested?

- ☐ Access to children
- ☐ Denial by adults close to the victim
- ☐ Reporting Challenges for Law Enforcement
- ☐ Lack of courage to intervene and act on suspicion
- ☐ Complicity by those in authority
- ☐ Ignoring 'red flags'

PROTECTING OUR CHILDREN FROM GROOMING

Victims between the ages of zero and 17 account for 67% of all reported sex crimes in the United States. These are our children. The greatest number of reported crimes will be perpetrated against adolescents and teens ages 12 - 17, followed by ages 6-11 and finally, ages 5 and younger.

Trust your gut and act on it! Sometimes parents can be afraid of how their child will react if they forbid the child from hanging out with a person he 'really' likes. Regardless of his initial reaction, it is important when you have concerns about a person's relationship with your child that you put an immediate stop to all contact between your child and the potential offender. It is also important to listen for statements or questions from your child that would support your suspicions, and to encourage your child to tell you more about the time he spends with the person. Be careful not to be accusatory, just interested and concerned.

Pie chart:
- 5 and younger: 14%
- 6-11: 20%
- 12-17: 33%
- 18-24: 14%
- 25-34: 12%
- 34+: 7%

Dr. Anna Salter, a renowned therapist who specializes in and interviews sex offenders, authored a book titled Predators. She recommends the following:

"Try to make your child a challenging target.
Predators do not want a challenge.
They want a VULNERABLE child."

When looking for a child to 'groom', offenders look for easy targets – kids who need attention, love and the sense of belonging they do not get at home. When you take an interest in your child's life, **YOU BECOME THE DETERRENT!**

A watchful parent puts an Offender on notice!
"No opportunity; no abuse."

What do you think could help your child to look 'challenging' to a predator? _____
_____
_____

What do you think could cause your child to look 'vulnerable' to a predator? _____
_____
_____

We cannot look at the above statistics and ignore the problem. Child sexual abuse is an epidemic destroying lives. This epidemic must be urgently addressed. Prevention education is the answer. So here are some proven ways to protect your child, making him less vulnerable and being sure he is a deterrent:

- Establish a NO SECRETS policy with your child (refer to *Gracie Finds Her Voice* a children's book at angelasvoice.com, for help with younger children). There is a difference between secrets and surprises; remember, secrets are concealed, surprises are revealed.

- Teach them to say "NO!" Have your child practice shouting a guttural "NO!" and let them know it is ok to scream at an adult or other authority figure if he feels threatened or afraid.

- Teach kids rules of physical contact and never insist they have physical contact with anyone they do not want to – including hugging the relative or friend of whom they are unsure.

- Reduce or eliminate one adult/older adolescent – one child interaction – your child should spend minimal time alone with another adult or older adolescent outside your watchful eye.

- Know the Child Sexual Abuse policies of all organizations your child is involved with (school, recreation, service organizations, and houses of faith).

- Maintain open lines of communication and trust with your child.

- Question your child when he has interacted with adults and older adolescents. Find out how the child feels about the interaction and ask specifics about events of the time spent together.

- Watch for potential signs of Child Sexual Abuse and INTERVENE! It is better to prevent something from happening than wait until it is too late.

- Always BELIEVE your child and ADVOCATE on his behalf.

- Teach your child to use a buddy system. Three is even better than two, offenders are always looking to get the child alone .

- Remember the quotes from the offenders in the first chapter of the book? We must talk frankly and often to our children about "the birds and the bees" and not allow sex offenders to educate our children for us.

Refer to *Tough Talk To Tender Hearts* for more information on how to talk to your children about Child Sexual Abuse and healthy boundaries – available at **angelasvoice.com**

> **What steps would you be willing to take if you recognized warning signs in one of your own family members or friends?** _____
> _____
> _____

When you IGNORE or DEVALUE the symptoms or warning signs of an offender 'grooming' it may ALLOW the offender to continue unhindered, leaving long-term effects in all facets of a child's life.

THINGS TO LOOK FOR IN A POTENTIAL CHILD SEXUAL ABUSE OFFENDER

When attempting to identify someone as a potential offender, it is important to ask yourself questions. The following is a basic overview of sex offender traits to consider:

1. What kind of BEHAVIOR does he exhibit? Does he:

- Show more interest in children than adults?
- Work or volunteer with children's organizations?
- Offer to babysit or take your child out to give you a break?
- Spend time alone with children when no other parents are involved?
- Buy gifts or spend money on children he knows?
- Abuse children physically or verbally?
- Exert power and control in social settings?

Child Sexual Offenders are preoccupied with children and/or adolescents. Remember, not everyone who enjoys working with children is an offender. Be watchful, not paranoid.

2. What kind of RELATIONSHIPS does he have?

If he is married:

- Does the marriage seem to be secure?
- Does he appear to be more affectionate with children than with his spouse?
- Does he spend unusual amounts of time with children away from family?

If he is single:

- Does he date people his own age?
- Does he date at all?
- Does he show more interest in single parents?
- Does she show more interest in her date's children?

In the case of a male, you want to take a close look at his wife or girlfriend and their relationship status. No sign of affection and/or verbal abuse is a possible red flag.

3. What kind of FRIENDS does he have?

- Does he have friends his own age?
- Does he socialize with people his own age?
- Does he have an active and varied social life?
- Does his friendships with people mostly include those who have children (especially if they are childless all or part time)?
- Does he seem to have adolescent friends in a particular age bracket? (12-15, for example)

> **OFFENDER GENDER PREFERENCES:**
>
> **Child Sexual Offenders will have preferences, a certain 'type' they prefer. Watch to see if there are obvious similarities in the children and adolescents they are often around. Those who prey on younger children seem to have less gender preferences, but those who like older adolescents will usually be more drawn to one particular gender.**

POSSIBLE SIGNS A CHILD IS BEING 'GROOMED'

It is important to observe your child. We do this naturally, but often miss signs of trouble because we do not know what he means or we innocently mistake those signs for something else (moodiness, growing older, isolation, sadness, etc.). At Angela's Voice, we are encouraging you to increase your awareness by engaging in discussions and observations. Doing so may prevent your child from becoming a victim to an offender's 'grooming'.

1. **Begin regular discussions with your child, especially when they have spent time away from you in the presence of adults and older adolescents.**
   As you listen and ask questions about their activities and interactions, does he:
   - Struggle to explain activities?
   - Search for the words when asked about a person?
   - Act afraid to speak or nervous to share?
   - Appear embarrassed or ashamed?
   - Give you a prepared answer when questioning them about a particular adult?
   - Have a contrary facial expression, telling a different story than his/her words suggest?
   - Resist interaction with a particular adult or older adolescent?

2. **Observe your child's behavior, moods, emotions and body.**
   Does he or she:
   - Have a sudden change in behavior?
   - Act isolated and emotionally disconnected?
   - Show signs of sleep disturbance or nightmares?
   - Draw pictures of bodies or sexual acts?
   - Have a sudden fear of people or places? Phobic responses?
   - Engage in sexual acts with other kids their age?
   - Have unusual stains or tears in their underwear?
   - Show signs of bruising, pain, genital discomfort or infections?
   - Wet the bed?

- Exhibit a change in eating habits, e.g., vomiting, eating strange foods?
- Have unusual fear of or is obsessed with bathing?
- Suffer from mood swings, depression?
- Show signs of self-harming behaviors (cutting, high risk behaviors)?
- Engage in violent behavior?
- Have promiscuous speech and/or behavior?
- Have an excessive curiosity about sex and/or masturbation?

CHILD SEXUAL ABUSE PREVENTION

Child Sexual Abuse PREVENTION is the responsibility of the adult, NOT the child. They are not equipped for the responsibility.

The key to minimizing the number of Child Sexual Abuse victims is PREVENTION. Prevention starts with awareness, paying attention to your child and those around your child, along with systems of protection for your family.

Here's what you can do:

- ☐ Learn the facts about Child Sexual Abuse – how and where it happens, who is vulnerable.
- ☐ Put systems in place to protect your children – inside your home and outside.
- ☐ Keep your eyes and ears open when it comes to your child.
- ☐ Pay attention to small details about your child, behavior and attitudes when it comes to those they spend time with.
- ☐ Trust your instincts; better to err on the side of caution.
- ☐ Do not disregard 'red flags' – explaining away concerns that should be noted.
- ☐ REPORT when you SUSPECT, and let the professionals investigate – there are protections in place for those who report.
- ☐ Protect your child regardless of who the suspected abuser is to you – brother, father, husband, grandfather, best friend, aunt, or uncle.

Place a checkmark next to each of the categories above where you think you need improvement. Remember, help is available if you need it and it is never too late to start prevention.

DEFINE ONLINE SOLICITATION BY PREDATORS

Our worlds are much bigger now that we have access to the worldwide web. Child Sexual Offenders are using the internet as a way to groom their victims with a greater ability to hide.

> "An online sexual solicitation is defined as an online communication where someone on the Internet tried to get [a minor] to talk about sex when they did not want to, an offender asked a minor to do something sexual they did not want to, or other sexual overtures coming out of online relationships."
>
> Finkelhor, Mitchell & Wolak, 2000

ONLINE STATISTICS

From the Crimes Against Children Research Center:

- 1 in 5 U.S. teens who regularly log on to the Internet say they have received an unwanted sexual solicitation via the Web
- 1 in 4 children have been exposed to unwanted pornographic material online
- 3 out of 4 children who encountered a sexual approach or solicitation did NOT tell an adult
- 1 in 33 youth received an aggressive sexual solicitation in the past year
- This means a predator asked a potential victim to meet somewhere, called him on the phone and/or sent the young person correspondence, money or gifts through the U.S. mail
- 77% of the targets for online predators were age 14 or older
- 22% were ages 10-13

According to these five statistics, 20% of U.S. teens have been the recipients of unwanted sexual advances online, an astonishing 75% of them did NOT tell an adult it happened. In the era of Internet and technology, the ability of a PREDATOR to make contact with a child is heightened. Education and vigilance are necessary to protect your child.

Which of the above numbers do you find most shocking? _____
_____
_____

A MODERN DAY PREDATOR PHENOMENA

According to Mitchell et al., 2005 (a study of sexual abuse against children), U.S. law enforcement studies found 44% of Internet initiated sex crimes were committed by FAMILY MEMBERS and 56% of the online PREDATORS were people known to the victim offline (friends, family, acquaintances, etc.)

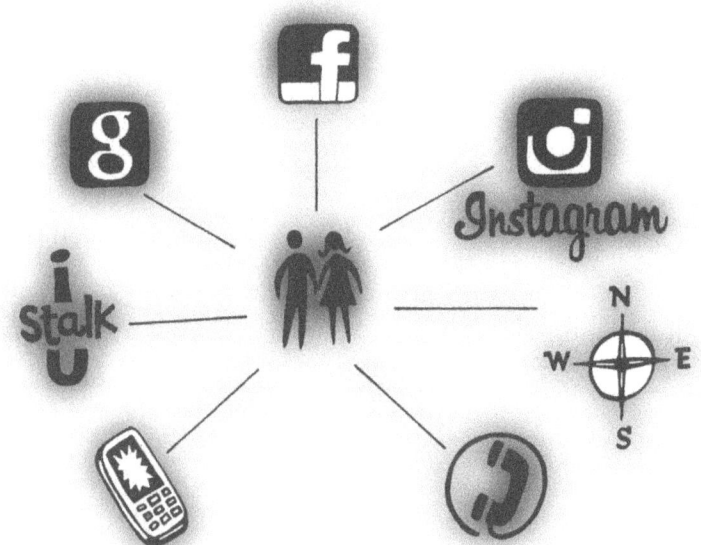

Online 'grooming' is rather insidious by virtue of being hidden behind a computer. The chances for detection are much smaller, requiring law enforcement to jump through hoops to get evidence on suspects. With the ability to change IP addresses, establish false identities and do so repeatedly, PREDATORS can evade detection unless they continue to commit or escalate their Internet sexual crimes.

Social Networking sites provide a large population of young people as potential targets, while safeguarding identities, even from law enforcement. User 'profiles' of millions can be viewed instantly from the privacy of a PREDATOR'S location, giving him the necessary information to determine potential victims.

The popularity of social media sites like FaceBook, Instagram, TikTok, etc., coupled with location tracking for computers, phones and gaming devices, has created open information 'sharing' of personal details, photos and locations. In an instant, a PREDATOR can access a child's name, address, school and even current location – which makes accessing a child in person, quickly, far more simple.

It cannot be stressed enough how important it is to instill wisdom in your children as they navigate the world of cyber space, and to be aware of what your child is doing on his computer, laptop, I-Pad, mobile phone, etc. Children need to be helped to understand to never give out personal, identifying information.

Which of the following does your child participate in:

- ☐ My Space
- ☐ Twitter
- ☐ Pinterest
- ☐ LinkedIn
- ☐ Facebook
- ☐ Flickr
- ☐ YouTube
- ☐ DeviantArt
- ☐ Google+
- ☐ Instagram
- ☐ TikTok
- ☐ MyLife

> **Do you know which of these sites and privacy controls to use to keep your child's information safe?** _____
>
> **And, which of these sites do not have adequate privacy controls?** _____

There is enough personal information posted on any of these sites for a PREDATOR to identify a vulnerable child or teen just by observing data and pictures. Be sure you have all access to every site your child visits or posts on and check it frequently. Angela's Voice recommends you review additional internet safety practices for children at Internet Safety 101 (internetsafety101.org).

INTERNET 'GROOMING' BEHAVIORS

Online PREDATORS are very sneaky, so detection takes more work. It is important to train yourself and your child to be sensitive to seemingly innocent clues as well as the more overt sexual ones. It is critical you consistently monitor your child's internet usage and online conversations.

Predators will become fast friends, building trust quickly. They do this by pretending to have a lot in common with your child. They will seem to share many likes and dislikes, mimicking the child's posts and comments.

They may or may not reveal their real identity. Since 75% of children do not tell an adult about online solicitations, offenders know they are not likely to be investigated and may be bold enough to use their real identity.

The offender may or may not be an adult. The larger number of online sexual solicitations comes from those of peer age. He will coerce a youth into sexualized discussions gradually, beginning with complimenting and flirting. The predator may send gifts in the mail to the child's home without a parent or guardian realizing that the gift is part of grooming the child. **This is especially easy if both parents are at work when the child returns home from school.**

A private cell phone may be purchased and provided to a potential victim so the offender can have communication that is undetected by parents or guardians. Vigilantly pay attention to the electronic devices your child uses. Do they have a phone or computer device you did not purchase and are not monitoring?

Offenders may or may not transmit sexual images of themselves or others and a sexual image is not necessary for a cyber-sexual crime to have taken place.

A solicitation to meet offline and have sexual contact may be part of the online interaction

There is a potential for harassment and threats to secure the child or teen into secrecy and compliance.

> Can you see how easily these behaviors can take place online? _____
> _____
> _____
>
> Can you also see how easily some of these behaviors could be overlooked or disregarded by you or your child until the situation escalates? _____
> _____

POSSIBLE SIGNS YOUR CHILD IS BEING 'GROOMED' VIA THE INTERNET

If your child is being preyed upon online, there may be obvious signs or behaviors to let you know. Keep your eyes and ears open to the following clues about your child:

- ☐ Spends a lot of time online, willing to forgo once loved activities and friends.
- ☐ Wants to spend his time on the Internet in private, insisting on seclusion from watchful eyes.
- ☐ Uses a webcam in private – this should never be allowed in your home or another.
- ☐ Does not allow parent or guardian access to phone, electronics, computer.
- ☐ Conceals porn or porn sites on his computer – this is very serious and intervention needs to take place immediately. Porn and those associated with porn can have very dangerous intentions where children and teens are concerned.
- ☐ Receives phone calls, gifts or mail from people you do not know. This can indicate an offender has detailed information regarding your child's or teen's whereabouts.
- ☐ Becomes withdrawn socially and in the home.
- ☐ Switches email or Instant Messaging accounts and/or changes passwords. If you previously had access to their electronics, computer and accounts, but cannot view them now, this maybe a reason to ground him from use of the equipment.
- ☐ Clears the 'browsing history' on the computer – so you cannot see what sites they have visited or searched for.
- ☐ Engages in more sexualized talk – especially if it seems inappropriate for his age and sexual growth.
- ☐ Lies about or hides Internet usage, cell phone and texting history to time and activities outside the home. Be on the lookout for any sudden or drastic change.

Please check any of the above possible indicators you have observed in your child.

> If you have noticed any of the indicators above and have intervened, what were the results? _____
> _____
> _____
>
> **Did the intervention stop the behavior?** _____
> _____
> _____
>
> **Did you find someone was involved with your child who raised your suspicion? If so, did you contact an appropriate agency to report?** _____
> _____
> _____
> _____

A NEW LANGUAGE

The rise of the Internet, Social Networking (SN), Texting, emails and other Instant Messaging (IM) forums have brought with them a new language, one using abbreviations for the sake of brevity in this fast-paced culture. Surely we all know what LOL (laugh out loud), OMG (oh my god), BRB (be right back) and ROTFL (rolling on the floor laughing) mean. Our written conversations are full of them. While these may seem simple to decipher, others may require assistance.

> Do you know what ASL means?_____
> _____

It means Age/Sex/Location and is posed as a question by those who do not know each other personally outside of the Internet. Part of protecting children is being aware of their conversations and intervening when something does not look right. But, you have to know their 'language' before you can spot what may be wrong.

INSTANT MESSAGING ABBREVIATIONS

This short list was provided by Netlingo, Connecting With Kids and www.missingkids.com. You are encouraged to refer to them or do your own search for further information. It is vital to be aware of some more common terms your child may be exposed to online. Please note some abbreviations may be offensive but all the more reason you must know and understand them.

ADR – Address

CTC – Choking the chicken (male masturbation)

EWI – Emailing while intoxicated

GALGAL – Give a little, get a little

IRL – In real life

KPC – Keeping parents clueless

MWBRL – More will be revealed later

NIFOC – Naked in front of computer

PAL – Parents are listening

PAW – Parents are watching

RUMORF – Are you male or female

TDTM – Talk dirty to me

TMTOWTDI – There's more than one way to do it

BWO – Black, white or other

DYFM – Dude you fascinate me

F2F – Face to face

IPN – I'm posting naked

IWSN – I want sex now

NAZ – Name, address, zip

NP – Nosy parents

PANB – Parents are nearby

POS – Parents over shoulder

STM – Spank the monkey (masturbation)

WTGP – Want to go private (message)

INTERNET 'GROOMING' PREVENTION AND PROTECTION

As with any form of prevention and protection, protecting kids online starts with awareness, dialogue with children and implementing systems to keep kids safe. The Internet requires all guardians of children to pay more attention than usual, due to its somewhat mysterious nature. Remember, pay attention and stay close to your children when they are using electronics of any kind. All Internet and usage should be in public areas.

Set up strict guidelines for Internet and electronics usage outside your home. Make sure your child knows the standard for them remains the same at someone else's home as well. You will need to have conversations with other parents or guardians to find out what their policy is at their home and make decisions accordingly. If you explain why you put the rules into play, they are more likely to follow your rules.

Never allow unsupervised usage of a webcam.

Teach your child how to keep themselves safe. You must teach your child what NOT to post online. We suggest not posting information like address, school name, sports team names, where they may be traveling, etc. All these give Offenders location indicators.

Equip all computers and electronics with parental monitoring software

For more information on Parental monitoring software recommended by Partner Organization Enough is Enough please visit this site: http://www.internetsafety101.org/filteringandmonitoring.htm

Know and monitor all passwords for devices and sites. If your child disobeys your rules, we recommend setting new passwords only you know, requiring you to be present to log on for them until they can be trusted again.

Know your child's Internet 'friends'. Do not allow them to have strangers or friends of 'friends' on their social media pages. This is how Offenders gain access.

Regularly log on to their electronics and sites to see what your child is posting and searching for online.

Be vigilant about pornography exposure. Pornography is highly addictive and dangerous. Once an addiction manifests, it becomes simpler for offender trafficking in pornography and sex to establish contact with potential victims. A little known fact: Pornography depresses people, so if your child starts showing signs of depression, think about checking his computer history.

Continue to seek education through workshops, programs and books. Angela's Voice offers several Internet/Cyber safety resources.

Teach your children about Internet safety, but keep in mind: Protection is your job!

Each member of your family should sign an Internet Safety Pledge. Please visit http://www.internetsafety101.org/youthpledge.htm for samples. For more information on sex offender Internet safety, contact Angela's Voice.

INTERNET 'GROOMING' INTERVENTION

As with other intervention or information gathering for the purpose of seeking civil or criminal justice, documentation is important. The Internet brings with it the ability to erase information quickly. Though it is always stored somewhere, law enforcement may not have the resources to dig more deeply. Your tracking of information could make the difference in developing or furthering a case.

Check what is on your child's computer, phone or other electronic devices

Track phone call and text records

With whom is your child communicating?
Do you know them?

Talk with your child if you have suspicions about him or someone else. Reiterate the dangers of online sex offenders.

Contact law enforcement immediately if you believe your child is at risk. Provide them with whatever documentation you may have. Be honest. Let them do the rest. Continue to document as necessary. Sometimes you need more than one incident to get legal intervention.

Keep these questions in mind, has your child:

- Asked to take an online relationship offline?
- Received pornography or abusive images? Print or photograph them if you can. They may be needed.
- Sexually solicited or received sexually explicit images from someone?
- Received any threats or coercion?

Keep detailed records of anything you find for law enforcement, even if it seems irrelevant.

THE VICTIM IS NEVER AT FAULT!

The heinous acts of Child Sexual Abuse are crimes and need to be investigated. If a child discloses something like this to you, remain calm. Your first step should be to affirm your child! If he has been victimized in person or on the Internet, he will be frightened and confused. PREDATORS will convince the child or teen he is complicit, or 'wanted it'. You will reverse this shame by letting your child know you believe him. Questions like "what were you thinking?" or "what did you do to cause this?" have NO place in a conversation with your child, especially if he has been brave enough to disclose. In addition to reporting this crime to law enforcement, you can consult a qualified mental health professional who can talk with you about what how to best help your child.

There is only one person at fault in these situations and it's the PREDATOR!!

DISCLOSURE – UNDERSTANDING THE PROCESS

- Child Sexual Abuse is a CRIME! **IMMEDIATELY CALL 911!**
- Always Report Suspicions of Child Sexual Abuse
- While seeking justice by reporting to authorities, advocate for the child.
- Let authorities manage the situation, while you care for the child.
- Say: "I believe you, and I will do everything I can to protect you. You did the right thing by telling me. I'm proud of you. This is not your fault."

The following pages relate to disclosure by an abused child.

CALMLY RECEIVING A DISCLOSURE

- Listen to the child carefully and write down what you hear so that you can report the facts to the authorities.
- Do not coach the child, do not suggest answers.
- Do not ask questions seeking more information. Let the child talk freely of his or her own volition. Children typically repeat the story accurately one time.
- Document what your child says.
- Report everything you know, even if, and especially, if the predator is in your home.
- Let authorities manage the situation.

FOLLOWING A DISCLOSURE

- Immediately remove your child from the dangerous environment.
- Report to local law enforcement or child protective services.
- Contact a local Child Advocacy Center for guidance.
- Use and depend on help of others.
- Understand a formal investigation will occur before any action is taken.
- Be courageous and advocate for the child.

BE AWARE AND PREPARE

- You will probably be required to provide a statement of what the child told you.
- Use what you wrote down and be specific.
- The justice system may be frustrating with long waits or professionals who may not be immediately responsive.

FOCUS ON THE FACT THAT YOUR CHILD IS NOW SAFE

- Children are frequently asked to testify in cases of sexual abuse. Do not be afraid or shy about procuring counseling for your child, yourself, or your family. Professional help is vital to recovery.

CHILD ADVOCACY CENTERS

Child Advoacy Centers are child friendly central locations for trauma intervention that may provide some or all of these services:

> - Crisis Services: Intervention, Assessment, and Treatment
> - Forensic Services: Interviews and Evaluations
> - Mental Health Services: Evaluations, Examinations, Individual and Group Counseling
> - Medical Services: Examinations, Evaluations, and Referrals
> - Advocacy Services: Family and court advocacy

Gone are the days when the only threat we teach our children is about strangers. We know that 93% of the threat is from someone the child knows and trusts. Having more information about sex offenders and the grooming process will better equip you to protect your child. Studies indicate that only 1 in 10 children will ever tell, so it is critical that we prepare ourselves with the necessary education to predict and prevent child sexual abuse in our homes, communities, youth service organizations and faith centers. As survivors find their voices, the numbers grow and we must be prepared to help them heal. We applaud you as a concerned adult who seeks the necessary training to help prevent child sexual abuse and help survivors disclose. Informed and confident children will result in reducing the threat of child sexual abuse. Thank you for joining the movement to protect the next generation of children.

RESOURCES:

CDC

US Department of Health and Human Services – Child Welfare division

"The Juvenile Sex Offender" by Howard Barbaree, 1993

Federal Bureau of Investigations

US Department of Justice, Center for Sex Offender Management

US Department of Justice, "Understanding Sex Offenders: An Introductory Curriculum"

US Department of Justice "Child Victimizers: Violent Offenders and Their Victims", 1996

childsafetyforparents.com

Snyder, 2000

Protecting the Gift by Gavin DeBecker

Finkelhor, Mitchell & Wolak, 2000

Crimes Against Children Research Center

Mitchell et al, 2005

www.netlingo.com

www.missingkids.com

www.connectingwithkids.com

Child Abuse and Neglect journal

www.nydailynews.com/blogs/iteam/2012/10/judge-john-clelands-statement-on-jerry-sandusky-sentencing

www.vachss.com/guest_dispatches/grooming.html

www.sikhhelpline.com/tag/bullying-stories/

ANGELA'S VOICE

Angela's Voice is dedicated to developing, distributing, and endorsing valuable resources in the awareness, prevention, and healing of child sexual abuse. The materials, though specific for survivors of child sexual abuse, also benefit any abuse survivor and help protect children by teaching them how to defend themselves from abusive behavior. Founder Angela Williams, MFP, is a survivor-turned-advocate who shares a powerful message of triumph over tragedy by sharing her vulnerable and candid voice about her abuse trauma, her pain, her struggles, and her journey to healing in hopes that it may help other survivors expedite their healing journey.

Williams has devoted years to providing awareness, prevention, and healing programs through her advocacy work. Williams has captivated audiences with her powerful message of triumph over tragedy as a victim of childhood physical and sexual abuse. At age seventeen, she attempted suicide, and that day was the end of her torment and the beginning of a journey to healing. She is a crusader for change and dedicates her life to eradicate child sexual abuse. She holds a master's in forensic psychology with a concentration in child abuse. Williams is a powerful messenger, appearing in national and international news and documentaries. She has been successful in state legislative reform and national policy work and served on the Policy Committee of the National Coalition to Prevent Child Sexual Abuse and Exploitation. She has received numerous accolades and awards for her work, including her collection of books that have valuable lessons for survivors of all ages.

Please follow Angela Williams on social media and contact angelasvoice.com to book a speaking event or interview.

Books by Angela Williams

Loving Me: After Abuse
From Sorrows to Sapphires, Angela Williams's Memoir

Interactive Workbooks—Adults

Healing

Pathway to Healing, Guide to Healing
True Intimacy
Shattering the Shame
Unveiling Child Sexual Abuse

Prevention

Tough Talk to Tender Hearts
The Grooming Mystery
Single Parenting Solutions
Courage to Speak

Children's Books (Ages 5–10)
Gracie Finds Her Voice
Grant Gets His Shield
Gracie and Grant's Big Win
Gracie and Grant's Big Win Coloring Book
Find Your Voice Curriculum Book

Join the Angela's Voice Movement

Take action to break the silence and cycle of Child Sexual Abuse and Exploitation

HELP US SAVE THE NEXT GENERATION OF CHILDREN!

1. Be a Child Advocate
2. Donate at angelasvoice.com
3. Invite Angela Williams to Speak
4. Purchase another Angela's Voice Prevention or Healing Book

Discover more child sexual abuse prevention and healing resources at **angelasvoice.com** and follow angelasvoice in social media.

Instagram @Angelasvoice

Facebook @Angelasvoice

Twitter @Angelasvoice

Linkedin/angelasvoice

Angelasvoice.blogspot.com

Youtube.com/angelakwilliams

www.ingramcontent.com/pod-product-compliance
Lightning Source LLC
Chambersburg PA
CBHW040010080526
44586CB00028B/2951